Presenting the Princess

The decision to publish a book about chronic pain was
the easy part. That the dream team of Carolyn Gage and
Sudie Rakusin could meld expressive language and elegant
drawings into a mythic story about this heartbreaking
subject was a received gift for us at Headmistress Press. I
am thrilled to introduce readers to *The Princess of Pain*,
in which a woman journeys far and wide seeking to
understand her own suffering, while enduring many trials
and tribulations.

As a Nurse Practitioner, I have witnessed many patients
who live with severe and disabling pain; pain that makes it
difficult—at times impossible—to work, to sleep, to make
love, to feel hunger, to enjoy laughter, to travel or even
leave home, to keep friends, and perhaps most importantly,
to learn how to live with it. But unlike acute pain that
warns us of danger to the body, chronic pain serves no
purpose whatsoever. I think of it as a rogue central nervous
system gone awry. Perhaps it is simply a mistake the body
has made in good faith, but one that no longer serves any
purpose, and now cannot be undone.

Sadly, popular conversation about chronic pain tends
to sidestep the experience. Instead of bearing witness to
a person in pain, instead of listening with empathy, we
are more likely to hear chatter about pain's peripheral
landscape: Opioids and overdoses. Family members who
say *get over it.* Friends who explain suffering as karma from
a past life. Medical providers who give up on patients. Self-
help books offering snake-oil cures. It seems that chronic
pain is too difficult to talk about.

In *The Princess of Pain,* our narrator sets out on a wearying quest to find answers to why her body has become her enemy. She encounters the wisdom, fury, strength, love, and trickery of the ancient goddesses, yet repeatedly, she is disappointed in their responses. Not even goddesses have answers for her. The solution, after all, is to recognize that there is no reason for chronic pain, no blame to be laid, no choice about who might be its subject, no known cure for it. There is only an individual's ability to recognize her own and others' suffering as akin and from this sharing, to somehow create meaning. Creating meaning is about the most human act we can engage in. At our best, we do this by listening and bearing witness. Sharing this kernel of wisdom with other sufferers, along with their friends, families, and yes, medical providers, is what this book is about.

—Risa Denenberg co-founder of Headmistress Press

In Carolyn Gage's *The Princess of Pain* we go on a moving journey of discovery with a woman tortured by constant pain. She takes us along in her wheelchair, seeking peace, answers, and an end to her pain, as she visits goddesses from around the world. The goddesses, lusciously illustrated by Sudie Rakusin and richly described by Gage, provide the princess with many beautiful and terrifying truths. *The Princess of Pain* delves deep into myth and story in gorgeous detail, leading the reader and the princess to recognize our incredible purpose, showing us how to name it, and to take into our hands the mystery of ourselves and our universe in acceptance.

—Jen Rouse author of *Cake*

The Princess of Pain is deceptively simple and universally human. Gage's story engages the heart and mind, pulling the reader forward with hope and desire. Rakusin's illustrations absorb the reader—this is not a story you merely dip a toe in; it is full-bodied, immersive. Part-metaphor, part-hero's journey, it remains entirely original. It is a necessary story teaching necessary lessons that somehow avoids preachiness and moralizing. We find our way into the Princess' heart and see the hope in her apparent pessimism.
— Hilary Brown author of *When She Woke She Was an Open Field*

Carolyn Gage is one of our most courageous and innovative writers to come of age inside the lesbian feminist movement of our time. Throughout her prolific career, Gage has given voice to women missing or misrepresented in the literary canon. Whether a lesbian Joan of Arc regretting her service to the king or a Harriet Tubman arguing with her therapist, Gage's women startle us not only because they are unfamiliar, but because they ring so true. In *The Princess of Pain,* Gage once again lures us past our threshold of comfort as we journey through the interior landscape of a woman suffering with irremediable pain. Under the magic of Gage's crystalline prose and Sudie Rakusin's resonant illustrations, any residue impulses to blame or otherwise distance ourselves from human suffering are exposed as base and cruel when set beside Princess' heroic, clear-eyed refusal of false palliatives.
—Patricia Morgne Cramer co-editor *Virginia Woolf: Lesbian Readings*

Books by Carolyn Gage

Play and Short Story Collections

The Second Coming of Joan of Arc and Selected Plays
Nine Short Plays
Three Comedies
The Triple Goddess: Three Plays
Black Eye and Other Short Plays
Starting from Zero: One-Act Plays About Lesbians in Love
The Spindle and Other Lesbian Fairy Tales
The Very Short Plays

Feminist Thinking

Like There's No Tomorrow: Meditations for Women Leaving Patriarchy
Sermons for a Lesbian Tent Revival
Supplemental Sermons for a Lesbian Tent Revival
Hotter Than Hell: More Sermons for a Lesbian Tent Revival
Sermons for a Hot Kitchen from the Lesbian Tent Revival

Lesbian Theatre

Monologues and Scenes for Lesbian Actors: Revised and Expanded
More Monologues and Scenes for Lesbian Actors
Take Stage! How to Direct and Produce a Lesbian Play

The Princess of Pain

The Princess of Pain

Carolyn Gage

Drawings by
Sudie Rakusin

Sally Jane Books

ISBN 978-0-9995930-5-9

PUBLISHER
Sally Jane Books, an imprint of Headmistress Press
60 Shipview Lane
Sequim, WA 98382
Telephone: 917-428-8312
Email: headmistresspress@gmail.com
Website: headmistresspress.blogspot.com

The Princess

Once upon a time there was a princess, and this princess was in pain. She had not always been in pain, but that time seemed so long ago now, it was almost as if it were a dream.

Her pain was very great, and when people would ask her about it, she would tell them that it felt like hot coals inside her arms and her legs, that it never went away, that it was always there—sometimes worse, sometimes not as bad—but always, always there.

The pain was so great it hurt her to walk. It hurt her to move. She spent a great deal of time in her bed, and people had to do most of the things she used to do by herself. When she did move, she used a motorized wheelchair. The princess tried everything in order to get rid of the pain. She tried different foods, and she took different pills, and she called on different doctors—and they poked and they patted and they prodded, and then they drugged and they cut and they injected, but nothing did any good, and sometimes the things they did made her feel even worse.

And sometimes people didn't believe she was in pain, because they weren't in pain. And sometimes people got annoyed with her, because she wasn't getting better, and they wanted her to. And sometimes people said things so stupid, the princess couldn't believe they weren't embarrassed to be even thinking those things.

People would tell her that there were blessings in the pain. They would tell her there were lessons in her pain. They would tell her that she was creating it herself, because it was something she needed to experience. They would tell her that if she would think nice thoughts it would go away. And sometimes, even though they wouldn't say it, they secretly believed she must have done something very, very bad in another lifetime—or maybe even this one! And so gradually, the princess began to pull away from the friends she had, or they pulled away from her. And her new friends didn't stay very long. Pretty soon she was left all alone in her big bed with her books and her poetry and her drawings and her music—and, of course, her pain.

She was so unhappy, she decided to go hunt up the goddesses and ask them why this had happened to her and what they expected her to do about it.

So she packed a few apples and a tuna fish sandwich in a bag that she hung over the back of her chair, along with a big water bottle, and she set off in her wheelchair to find the goddesses.

Aphrodite

She had been riding for almost a quarter of an hour when she came to a grove of trees. There was a great cloud of steam rising from the grove, and the princess could hear the sound of a woman laughing. She turned down a little paved path, and there was her first goddess.

It was Aphrodite, the Greek goddess herself, naked as the day she rode in on the sea foam, frolicking in a pool of naturally heated mineral water! She was lying back, kicking her feet and throwing handfuls of water into the air to watch the sun catch the sparkling drops before they fell back on her laughing face.

"Aphrodite!" the princess called. She had to call her name several times, because the goddess was so absorbed in her pleasure. "Aphrodite! Aphrodite!"

Startled, the goddess turned in the direction of the

princess.

"Why am I in so much pain?"

Aphrodite looked at her and asked her how long it
had been since she had laughed. The princess said
it had been a while since she had had anything to
laugh about. And then Aphrodite invited her to
come down into the pool. The princess got out of her
wheelchair and slowly and painfully limped down to
the water. She took off her clothes and slid into the
warm waters. This was a difficult operation, and it
took her a few minutes before she could say anything.
Aphrodite watched her with interest.

"I can teach you about pleasure, but I don't know
anything about pain," said Aphrodite. "Then teach me
about pleasure," said the princess, and Aphrodite did.

She showed the princess how to touch herself and
how to touch another woman, and there was nothing

about pleasure she didn't teach her, and the princess experienced many delights that afternoon with Aphrodite, but the pain was always the same, even when Aphrodite kissed her—and it's no small thing to be kissed by the Goddess of Love.

And so the princess got out of the pool and put her clothes back on, and turned sadly away. Aphrodite went back to pleasuring herself, because the princess had left, and the Goddess of Love, as we know, has a notoriously short attention span.

Hecate

The princess wheeled back onto the main road and, in another quarter-mile or so, she arrived at a place where three roads came together. She didn't know where any of the roads went, but there was an old woman digging post-holes near the crossroads, and so the princess asked her which way she should go.

The old woman looked up, wiping the sweat from her eyes. "That depends on where you want to end up," she said.

"Anywhere I can get rid of my pain," said the princess.

"Ah, then it isn't going to matter which road you take."

The old woman turned back to her post-holes.

"Why not?" asked the princess. The old woman ignored her. "I said 'why not?'" persisted the princess. Again the old woman ignored her. "Are you saying I'm not going to get rid of my pain?"

When the old woman ignored her for the third time, the princess decided she must be some kind of philosopher or mystic, because they had a habit of saying things like that to her, and then acting like she didn't understand, when, in fact, the princess knew they were the ones who didn't understand. There wasn't much the princess hadn't heard, because of her pain.

And so she stopped trying to get the old woman's attention, and she picked the road that looked like it would be the easiest, because it went downhill, and off she went.

And downhill it was. The princess found herself going down and down and down and down, and when she thought the road couldn't possibly go down any farther, it would go down some more. And as it went down, it became darker and darker and warmer and warmer, and the princess began to realize that she was not outdoors anymore, but that she was down under the earth. And just when she had decided that maybe it was time to turn back, the road went around a bend and she saw a pool of lava glowing orange-red right in front of her!

Pele

She put on her safety brakes so suddenly, she was almost thrown out of the chair. Just then the pool of molten rocks became very agitated, sputtering and splattering, and suddenly a great fiery goddess rose up from the center of it. It was the Hawai'ian goddess Pele. The princess had somehow gotten herself into the heart of Kilauea Crater.

"Pain? Who speaks of pain to Pele?" The princess was too astonished to answer, and, frankly, she was a little concerned about the bits of lava that were landing within a few feet of her chair.

The lava streamed from Pele, revealing her long dark hair, but her eyes continued to glow like hot coals. "You come to speak to Pele of pain? What can you know of pain in a year, in two years?"

"It's been six years!" said the princess, her own fire

beginning to rise.

"Silence! I speak of the pain of hundreds, thousands, millions in pain, in slavery, hundreds of years. I speak of the rape of women, of their babies born dead from nuclear radiation, born into enslavement by the white men who have ravaged my land, my beautiful, beautiful land—these worms, these monsters, these white, crawling parasites! Pain? The loss of beauty, the loss of freedom, the loss of innocence—"

"But I have lost these things," said the princess.

"Silence—"

"Oh, 'silence,' yourself! I know what pain is! Maybe not your pain, but mine is enough, and if you really understood pain, you would understand that."

And Pele looked at her with those great glowing eyes, and she approved of what she saw.

"You must burn if you are to live with pain."

"But I don't want to burn, and I don't want to yell at you, and all I want is for this terrible pain to stop!"

But Pele was already descending back into her pool of lava. In the cave of the crater, the princess could hear the echo of her last words, "You must burn… You must burn… You must burn… "

The princess was very angry, and she was frightened at being so angry. It's one thing for the Goddess of Fire to burn with rage, but the princess was only human, and a human can only stand to burn so much.

Baubo

And so she released the brakes and turned her back on the crater of Kilauea and began the long journey back to the surface of the earth. And although it was the same road, it was a harder road, because this time she was traveling uphill. It was just as much uphill as it had been downhill, but somehow, to the princess, it seemed many, many times steeper and longer than when she had been traveling downhill. And the princess found it was necessary to stop and rest, even though the chair was doing most of the work, because it was painful and tiring for her to be in motion at all.

And as soon as the princess stopped to rest, she started to cry. All of that anger and all of that effort, and all it was going to do was put her right back where she started from! And while she was crying, she didn't notice that a woman in a long dress had crept up beside her.

And suddenly, when the princess looked up, there was a woman standing right in front of her and asking if she would like to see the face of the bearded man.

"What?" asked the princess, wiping her nose.

"The face of the bearded man. Would you like to see it?"

"I don't know. What is it?" asked the princess.

"It's this," said the woman, and before the princess knew what was happening the woman had reached down to the hem of her dress, grabbed it, and lifted the whole thing up over her head. Underneath the dress, the woman was buck-naked!

And, sure enough, there were her two nipples like large, brown eyes, and below them, the biggest, silliest clown smile painted across her belly—and it was true: Her naked body really did look like the face of a bearded man. The princess didn't know what to make of it. The whole situation was so ridiculous—one woman sitting there in her chair weeping and the other woman standing in front of her with her dress up over her head and her body looking like a clown face—that the princess began to laugh.

At the sound of the princess' laughter, the woman, who turned out to be another one of the Greek goddesses, put her dress down and introduced herself.

"I'm Baubo. I use that trick a lot, and it always makes women laugh. Can I have one of your apples?"

Baubo sat down on the ground and began to eat. "The other goddesses don't think much of me and my bearded-man's face, but who do you think it was that got the Earth Goddess Demeter out of her depression and back on her feet again after her daughter was kidnapped? Yours truly.

That's right. Demeter was even more depressed than
you. She wasn't even crying. She was just sitting. Just
sitting and not caring about anything, and she was
letting the whole planet go to seed, because she didn't
care about anything except her daughter who was
missing.

So I went up to her and I asked her, just like I asked
you, if she'd like to see the man with the beard… only
she didn't answer. She just sat there and kept staring.
So I showed her the man, just like I showed you, only
she didn't laugh. So I just kept standing there. So
there we were, me and Demeter… her just sitting and
staring, and me just standing there like an idiot with
my dress up over my head. But you know something,
after a while, she laughed. I mean, it wasn't a big
laugh… more like just a little snort-laugh. But it was
a laugh just the same, and that's what got her going
again. Yep. Got her going clear all the way down to
Hades, where her daughter was. Brought her back,
too. Want a bite?"

Baubo offered the apple to the princess. The princess held up her hand.

"Oh, go on. Take a bite. It's your apple."

The princess took a bite. Satisfied, Baubo continued her narrative. "Well, so now, when the goddesses say, 'Here comes Baubo with that stupid trick of hers,' I just remind them that if it hadn't been for me, there wouldn't be any trees, or flowers, or grass, or bushes."

"But I haven't lost my daughter," said the princess. "I'm in pain—terrible pain, all the time."

"What about when you were laughing at me?" asked Baubo.

"Even then."

Baubo looked puzzled. "Are you sure?"

"Very sure. It never goes away. Even when I sleep."

And then Baubo looked very sad. "Then, I don't think I can help you."

The goddess looked so sad, the princess almost wanted to pretend she felt better, but she didn't, and so she thanked Baubo for trying, and she rolled back onto the road that went uphill, back to the crossroads where the old woman had told her it wouldn't matter which road she took.

"And maybe it won't," thought the princess, "but I'm in pain whether I go or stay, so I may as well go."

I HAVE COME FROM AFAR

I AM ALL THAT HAS BEEN THAT IS AND THAT WILL BE . . . .

Athena

The old woman was still digging her post-holes and still ignoring the princess, so the princess rolled right past her without saying a word. This time, she picked a road that went neither up nor down, but out onto a wide, flat plain.

In the distance, she could see tiny figures, but they were so far away she couldn't make out what they were doing. As she got closer, she realized that they were women with swords and shields, and that they were practicing fighting with each other. Their leader was a very, very strong woman, not too tall, but with muscles you could see even when she wasn't using them.

She was busy coaching the women in their fighting skills, but she turned when one of the women cried out, "Look! A chariot without a horse! She rides a chariot without a horse!"

The warrior women left off fighting and gathered around the wheelchair with great curiosity. The princess took pride in showing them all how it worked, how she could make it go faster or slower, how she could make it back up, or turn to one side, or spin around in very small circles. She showed them the batteries (she carried a spare), the joystick, the electric horn, and the safety brakes. The women, used to the wooden wheels of chariots, marveled at the rubber tires. And they showed their approval for how the princess had fitted the back of the chair with a bag for her food and a bottle for her water.

The princess was just getting ready to show them how fast she could travel, when the leader suddenly clanged her sword against her shield. The women moved quickly away from the chariot-with-no-horse and formed themselves into a straight line. They stood very still, shoulder to shoulder, looking neither to the left, nor to the right.

The leader passed back and forth along the line, inspecting the women. Suddenly, she reached out with her sword and tapped one of the women on the top of her shoulder. The woman stepped out of the line, drew her sword, and began to spar with her teacher. Both the student and the teacher were very skilled, but the teacher was the quicker of the two, and it wasn't long before she had her student's sword on the ground.

The warrior women went back to the line, where the women were still in perfect formation. The leader tapped another student, and this woman stepped forward to spar. One by one, the teacher tested them. Finally, after the fourth woman had been defeated, the princess wheeled herself forward.

"Excuse me, but I would like to fight you."

Athena—for, of course, the goddess was Athena— looked at her very hard.

The princess did not have muscles like the other fighters. In fact, she did not have muscles even like non-athletic, but able-bodied women. Because of her pain, the princess had not been able to use her muscles for many years, and so they were not very big at all.

The great warrior goddess narrowed her eyes at the princess. "But you have never trained with me."

"I have never trained with you, it's true, but I have trained, and I would like to fight you."

Athena looked at the princess' arms. The princess lifted her chin ever so slightly.

"Can you use a sword?" asked the Goddess of War.

"I can use my wits and they're sharper than any sword, even yours."

And no sooner were those words out of her mouth, than Athena lunged for the princess' neck, but the princess was even quicker. She pushed the joystick forward, ramming the metal plates of the footrests into Athena's shins, and, at the same time, she ducked under Athena's arms and retrieved the canister of pepper spray that hung below the seat of the chair. Holding the spray in front of her with both hands, she aimed the canister directly toward her attacker's face and shouted "Back off!"

Athena cut swiftly to one side attempting to reach around behind the princess, but the princess twisted in her chair, and, this time, she released the pepper spray. Athena covered her face, but it was too late. Already the goddess was bent over with coughing. The princess took the whistle that hung on a chain around her neck, and blew as hard as she could. "Get help!" she cried. "Fire!" The warrior women stood in stunned silence for a moment, and then they began to cheer. The princess was still shouting, when Athena came and laid her sword at the princess' feet.

"You fight well," she said.

"I have to," the princess replied simply. "I live in pain all the time. I want you to teach me how to defeat my enemy."

Athena studied the princess' face. "You speak of your own body as an enemy?"

"I do. It is," said the princess.

"If you defeat your body, you will have killed yourself." Athena looked grim. "A warrior never, never takes her own life."

The princess looked at her solemnly. "Sometimes they do."

Athena and the princess looked hard at each other

in silence for a moment, and finally, Athena looked away. "It's true, but it's extreme."

"My pain is extreme."

Athena shook her head. "Only you can know what you can bear. I cannot help you, Brave One. You are perhaps the greatest warrior of them all."

And Athena knelt before the princess for the second time, and touched her forehead to the princess' feet. But the princess felt no joy in having defeated the Goddess of War. She had hoped that this would be the goddess to teach her how to kill her pain.

Fighting back her tears, the princess wheeled herself slowly back onto the road. Behind her, she could hear the sound of sword on shield as the women resumed their exercises.

Bastet

When she got to the crossroads this time, she was alone. The princess decided it would be a good idea to eat her lunch before she set out on the last road. She wasn't hungry, but that was not unusual for her. The pain made it difficult to feel hungry. She unwrapped the tuna fish sandwich, and began eating it very slowly.

Suddenly, she felt something brush against her leg. Looking down, she saw a large black cat.

"Oh, please go away," she said. "I'm allergic to cats." Already, she could begin to feel her throat closing up. "Go away! Shoo!"

But the cat was persistent, and as the princess had always been fond of cats before the disability, she reached down to pet the animal. Suddenly, to her amazement, the cat began to grow taller and taller.

What was even more amazing, the body seemed to absorb all of the fur and become the body of a woman—except for the head, which grew as large as a human head and remained that of a black cat.

It was Bastet, the Egyptian Goddess of the Home. The princess had never seen anything so odd-looking in her life, and she didn't know what to say. Fortunately, Bastet did.

"May I have your sandwich, if you're not going to eat it?"

The princess was too surprised to respond for a moment, but the cat-woman persisted: "May I?" The princess picked up what was left of the sandwich and held it out to Bastet.

"Do you want any more of it?" the cat goddess asked.

"You can have it." The princess really wasn't hungry at all.

Bastet took the sandwich in her woman-hands, and then bent her head down and began to eat the sandwich, cat-fashion, sniffing it and bumping it with her nose, and then taking the bread in her mouth and shaking it, so that the bits of tuna fish went flying. The princess, unsure of the protocol for such an encounter, reached up as discretely as she could to dislodge the chunks of tuna that had landed in her hair.

"Good," purred Bastet. "Make it yourself?"

"Yes," said the princess.

"You must be a good cook."

"Oh, I used to be, before I got sick. Now it's too painful for me to use my arms."

Bastet continued shaking and flinging the slices of bread while the princess spoke. "I had a cat, too. Her name was Willow, but now she has to stay outdoors, because I'm allergic to her."

Bastet paused between bites and made a sympathetic sound.

"It's hard to be at home in my home anymore. I have so many allergies and I can't do any of the things I used to." She sighed. "I don't suppose you can do anything about that."

Bastet had finished the tuna fish sandwich by now, and she was performing a very unusual operation, stroking her whiskers with her woman-hands and then licking them clean as if they were paws.

"Would you care for a napkin?"

Bastet was too busy licking to have heard the princess' offer, and the princess decided it was best not to repeat it. Finally Bastet was through with her

grooming. She turned her yellow eyes toward the
princess and said:

"A home is where you are used to things."

"But I never get used to the pain."

Bastet crouched down next to the princess and butted
her large head against the princess' shoulder. She
did it very gently, so as not to hurt her, and that way
the princess knew she was comforting her, the way
that cats have always comforted humans these many
thousands of years. A simple enough gesture, but it
was kinder and more direct than most of the things
humans would come up with in situations like this.

And after that, Bastet began to shrink again, until
she was just a large, black, Egyptian cat. The princess
sighed. Here was another goddess unable to help
her! She slowly wheeled away from the crossroads,
leaving the Goddess of the Home picking and pawing

through bits of tuna that somehow had gotten scattered on the ground.

The third road led to the ocean, and after a while, the princess could smell the salt spray in her nose. It had been so long, so very long since she had been to the ocean… another lifetime. And she had so loved the ocean, so loved running along the sand! Wheelchairs don't travel on the sand, she thought sadly. Wheelchairs don't travel anywhere beautiful or private, she thought.

Kwan Yin

The road led her up to the dunes, and there she was able to sit and look out over the ocean. She was able to hear the rhythmic roar of the waves on the beach. It was very soothing to be there. So soothing, in fact, that the princess began to fall asleep. She couldn't tell if she was dreaming or not when a great Asian goddess arose out of the surf and came toward her on the dunes.

This was Kwan Yin, the Chinese Goddess of Compassion.

As the princess lay slumped in her chair, her head nodding gently on her chest, Kwan Yin wrapped her soft robes about her and began to whisper words of comfort in her ear. The princess couldn't tell if it was the sound of the waves, or the sound of Kwan Yin breathing. She couldn't tell if it was the breeze blowing in from the ocean, or Kwan Yin's long fingers stroking the hair back from her forehead.

"Kwan Yin… Kwan Yin… " Was it the goddess
singing to her, or was she calling the goddess? "Kwan
Yin… Kwan Yin… " The princess was going deeper
and deeper into a trance. She could still feel the pain,
but it was as if it were in another place, as if the pain
were a huge roaring bonfire that she was walking away
from… walking away from.

"Kwan Yin… Kwan Yin… Kwan Yin… "

The great red sun began to slip down behind the
horizon, and the breeze began to grow colder and
colder, and suddenly the princess awoke with a start.
Had she been dreaming? Where had she been? Had
Kwan Yin really been with her?

The pain was acute in her arms and legs, because she
was cold.

"Oh, how will I be able to get back?" The princess began to panic. She felt so helpless sometimes in her wheelchair. It seemed so unfair that any time she indulged herself at all, there was always such a high price to pay.

The wind continued to rise, and the sky grew darker and darker. The princess pushed her chair to go faster and faster, and the faster it went, the more it bumped over the road and hurt her body, but she was determined to get back to where she had started as quickly as she could. Pretty soon it was very dark, and she could hardly see the road, but this only increased her sense of urgency. And before she had time to think, the wheelchair had run off the edge of the road and was stuck fast in the sand.

"Oh!" she cried out in her fear and frustration. And she got out of the chair, which was painful and difficult for her, and she began to tug at the heavy chair with two batteries. This was very painful on her arms, and she found she was unable to budge the chair. She kicked the wheels, and hit the arms of it, and now her hands hurt.

She sat in the lopsided chair with the cold wind blowing on her neck, and, tucking her hands under her armpits, she began to howl.

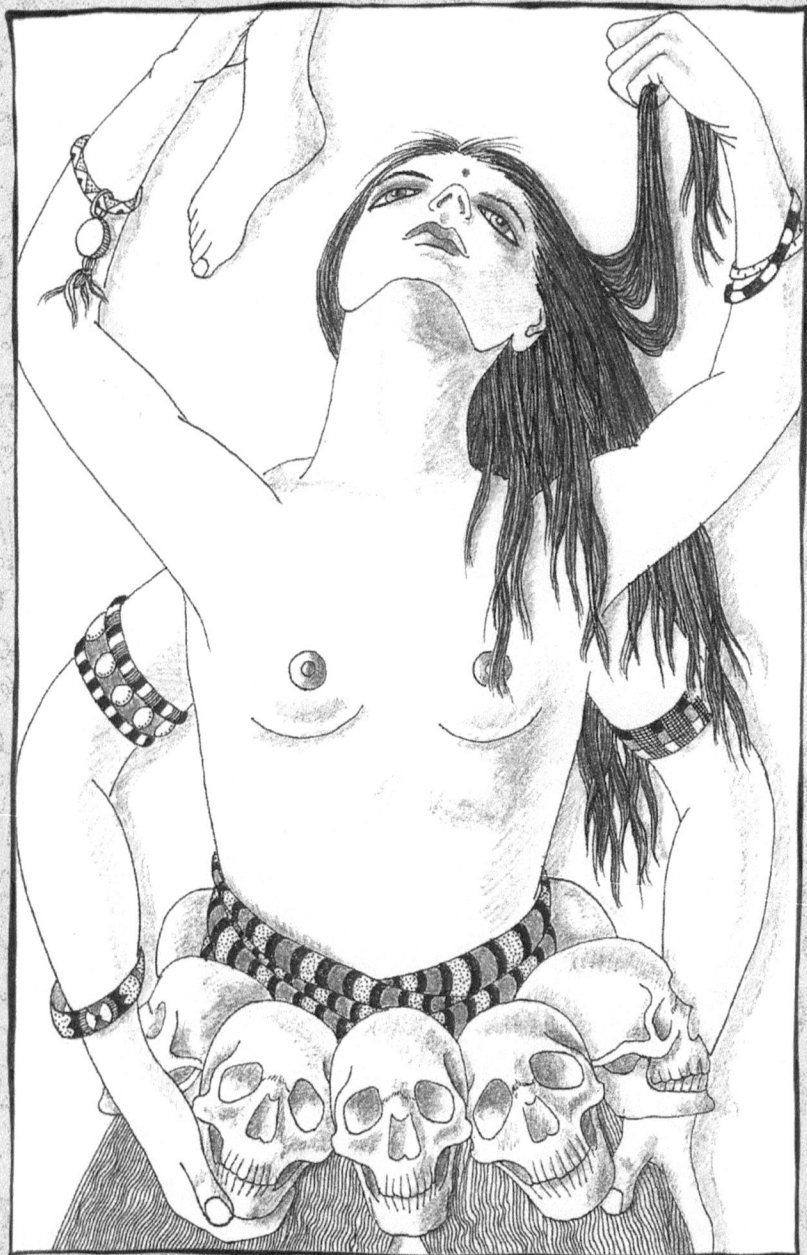

Kali

Suddenly a goddess appeared out of the dark. It was a goddess with four arms and a belt of human skulls. She also had a string of human arms and legs hanging around her waist, and she was eating her own intestines. It was Kali, the Destroyer Goddess of India.

The princess, too helpless and unhappy to be afraid, kept howling, and Kali, her mouth dripping with blood from her intestines, howled back at her and danced so that the dead arms and legs flapped around her hips. And the princess screamed, "You can take my arms and legs, too, for your belt. I hate them! I hate them!" And she began to pull at her legs, trying to tear them off, but, of course, they stayed firmly attached to the rest of her body.

And Kali laughed at the princess, and rattled her skulls, which only made the princess howl more.

She began to curse the Goddess of Destruction. She cursed her with every word she knew, at the top of her lungs. She cursed her, and then she cursed her own body. She cursed her arms and legs that burned all the time like hot coals. She cursed her wheelchair, kicking at it while she did. She cursed her circulation, her nervous system, her muscles. She cursed the doctors who couldn't help her, she cursed the people who said such stupid, stupid things to her, she cursed the goddesses who didn't answer her questions, and then she began to curse her own stupidity in thinking there would be any answers, any cure, any help, any hope. She cursed herself for not knowing it was her fate to be tortured more than other people, to live in the kind of pain all day and all night that most people would find unbearable for five minutes. She laughed a wild laugh at her impossible stupidity for believing she had any right to anything, to any love, to any comfort, to any peace, to any safety, to any rest. And Kali laughed and taunted and shook her bones at her while she cursed.

And then she cried. She cried because it was freezing cold, but she knew it was not cold enough to kill her, and that all that would happen would be what had always happened: She would suffer, and her suffering would just be more and more and never less, and this would go on as long as she was willing not to kill herself. And she knew that, in spite of it all, she wasn't ready to die, and so she would just go on suffering, and great tears rolled down her cheeks.

Yemanja

And gradually the sound of Kali's bones faded into the night, and the wind died down, and a soft murmur arose between the sounds of the waves. It was a woman's voice, a soft, rich voice, like a humming song from way deep in the throat.

And the princess looked up to see the great African goddess, Yemanja. Suddenly, the princess was no longer in her wheelchair. She was no longer on the dunes. She was in the bosom of the Mother of the Earth, and the Mother of the Earth was teaching her.

The princess heard Yemanja tell her about birthing, about how the great waters of the ocean flowed from Yemanja's amniotic sack when she was giving birth to the world. Yemanja talked about her labor, her agony, and she talked about the enslavement and torture of her people and the suffering they knew they would not escape in a lifetime, and that their children would not escape in their lifetime, nor their children's children.

She talked about hatred, and how some of her people would turn their anger on their own children and on themselves. She told the princess that there was no justice in the world, no compensation for the suffering, no cures for the inequality in the world. She told of her sorrow and her rage at how it had all turned out, for the world was bigger than the goddesses, and she told her that she, the princess, would have to answer her own questions, find her own meaning—that her life was a terrible ordeal, and that there was no purpose to her suffering, no reason for her being the one to suffer.

And the princess had known these things all along, and so it was good, even though it was hard, to hear them. Yemanja understood, and that was a relief to the princess.

And in the arms of Yemanja, she found she could see with the eyes of Yemanja. And as the great sun rose again over the earth, the princess saw the pain and the horror of poisoned air and water, the boneyards of the massacres of millions upon millions of people by the men of every race and color and nationality. She saw the diseases, the poverty, the starvation, the misery— the utter misery of the creatures on the planet, and she could not accept it, but it still just was.

And when the sun had risen, she looked down and saw the dunes below her, and there was her wheelchair, still lying tilted in the sand. Yemanja set the princess gently down beside it, and then she turned and disappeared into the ocean.

The princess sighed. She knew that she would have to get the chair out of the sand, and that, in order to do this, she would have to take everything off of it so as to make it as light as possible, and she knew she would have to take the heavy batteries off, and then lift them back on again. And she knew she would have to dig and dig in the sand, and that it might take her all day to get the chair back on the road, and that all of this would be very painful and take a very long time.

The princess sighed. She took out her water bottle and her last remaining apple. She thought of Baubo, and she thought of Bastet, and she thought of Aphrodite kissing her, and of Athena saluting her, and she remembered the kindness of Kwan Yin, and the fury of Pele, and the tauntings of Kali, and the wisdom of Yemanja, and then she remembered the woman at the crossroads and wondered if she would see her again on her way back home.

She sighed and bit into the apple, thinking to herself, "And I must be the Goddess of Pain."

And so she was.

Headmistress Press Books

Riding with Anne Sexton - Jen Rouse

Seed - Janice Gould

The Princess of Pain - Carolyn Gage, Sudie Rakusin

She/Her/Hers - Amy Lauren

Spoiled Meat - Nicole Santalucia

Cake - Jen Rouse

The Salt and the Song - Virginia Petrucci

mad girl's crush tweet - summer jade leavitt

Saturn coming out of its Retrograde - Briana Roldan

i am this girl - gina marie bernard

Week/End - Sarah Duncan

My Girl's Green Jacket - Mary Meriam

Nuts in Nutland - Mary Meriam, Hannah Barrett

Lovely - Lesléa Newman

Teeth & Teeth - Robin Reagler

How Distant the City - Freesia McKee

Shopgirls - Marissa Higgins

Riddle - Diane Fortney

When She Woke She Was an Open Field - Hilary Brown

God With Us - Amy Lauren

A Crown of Violets - Renée Vivien tr. Samantha Pious

Fireworks in the Graveyard - Joy Ladin

Social Dance - Carolyn Boll

The Force of Gratitude - Janice Gould

Spine - Sarah Caulfield

I Wore the Only Garden I've Ever Grown - Kathryn Leland

Diatribe from the Library - Farrell Greenwald Brenner
Blind Girl Grunt - Constance Merritt
Acid and Tender - Jen Rouse
Beautiful Machinery - Wendy DeGroat
Odd Mercy - Gail Thomas
The Great Scissor Hunt - Jessica K. Hylton
A Bracelet of Honeybees - Lynn Strongin
Whirlwind @ Lesbos - Risa Denenberg
The Body's Alphabet - Ann Tweedy
First name Barbie last name Doll - Maureen Bocka
Heaven to Me - Abe Louise Young
Sticky - Carter Steinmann
Tiger Laughs When You Push - Ruth Lehrer
Night Ringing - Laura Foley
Paper Cranes - Dinah Dietrich
On Loving a Saudi Girl - Carina Yun
The Burn Poems - Lynn Strongin
I Carry My Mother - Lesléa Newman
Distant Music - Joan Annsfire
The Awful Suicidal Swans - Flower Conroy
Joy Street - Laura Foley
Chiaroscuro Kisses - G.L. Morrison
The Lillian Trilogy - Mary Meriam
Lady of the Moon - Amy Lowell, Lillian Faderman, Mary Meriam
Irresistible Sonnets - ed. Mary Meriam
Lavender Review - ed. Mary Meriam

www.ingramcontent.com/pod-product-compliance
Lightning Source LLC
Chambersburg PA
CBHW071240090426
42736CB00014B/3163